Building History
ROMAN VILLA

Gillian Clements

W
FRANKLIN WATTS
LONDON • SYDNEY

First published in 2004 by
Franklin Watts
96 Leonard Street
London
EC2A 4XD

Franklin Watts Australia
45-51 Huntley Street
Alexandria
NSW 2015

Editors: Rachel Cooke and Sally Luck
Art Director: Jonathan Hair
Consultant: Francis Grew, Curator of
Archaeology, Museum of London

ISBN: 0 7496 5139 3

A CIP catalogue record for this book is
available from the British Library.

Printed in Malaysia

 Contents

6-7   What is a Roman villa?

8-9   What was the Roman Empire?

10-11   What was life in the Empire like?

12-13   Why build yourself a villa?

14-15   Where did you build your villa?

16-17   Who were the builders?

18-19   How were the villas built?

20   How were the villas heated?

21   What were Roman baths?

22-23   How did you decorate your villa?

24-25   How did you live in your villa?

26-27   What happened to the Empire?

28   Timeline

29   Glossary

30   Index

What is a Roman villa?

Many centuries ago well-to-do Romans lived in large, comfortable country houses called villas. The Romans had seen wonderful architecture in Ancient Greece and they adapted some of these ideas to create their own luxurious homes.

What were Roman villas like?

Few of these country homes were exactly alike. One family's villa could be a simple working farmhouse which supplied food to a nearby town. Another could be a huge luxurious house close to Rome – a quiet hill retreat for its wealthy owner to get away from the city. However, although they could look quite different from the outside, villas had many things in common – mosaic floors, courtyards with columns and luxurious bathhouses offering cold, warm and hot water.

Archaeologists have found the remains of about 600 villas in southern Britain alone.

Who were the villas for?

Many different kinds of people chose to live in a villa. In Italy, they were for rich Roman citizens. Elsewhere non-Romans, who had done well under Roman rule, built villas too. These non-Romans may have been wealthy farmers, tradesmen or businessmen.

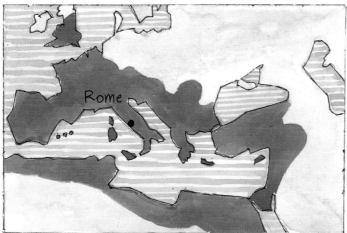

◀ The red colour shows the extent of the Roman Empire at its largest, in AD117.

Where did they build the villas?

The Romans first built these villas at home in Italy, in the countryside surrounding the major towns like Rome and Pompeii. The owners wanted to live on good farming land and be close to towns and markets. As the Roman Empire grew, villas were built in nearly all the conquered countries.

When did they build the villas?

Wealthy Romans were building villas in the 2nd century BC. By this stage, their army had already begun to conquer Rome's huge empire. It continued to conquer new territories for the next 400 years. Villas were built during the whole of this time.

What was the Roman Empire?

Rome is a city in Italy which, tradition says, was founded by Romulus in 753BC. Over the centuries, Rome's power grew. Its people eventually conquered most of Italy, Europe and parts of North Africa and the Middle East. These lands made up the Roman Empire.

① Spain

In 206BC Rome defeats Hannibal of Cathage's armies – and his elephants –and takes control of southern and eastern Spain.

② Greece

Philip of Macedon is heavily defeated in 197BC. Fifty years later, Greece and Macedonia become part of the Roman Empire.

③ Carthage

In 146BC Rome finally defeats this powerful state and destroys the city. Carthage had ruled parts of Africa's north-west coast, Corsica and Sicily. Rome now rules these lands as well.

④ Asia Minor

Between 133 and 130BC Rome seizes power in western Turkey and creates the province of Asia. Later, the Empire will be extended eastwards across the whole of what is now the country of Turkey.

⑤ Gaul (France)

Rome conquers southern Gaul in 121BC. During the 50s BC, Julius Caesar's army conquers the north.

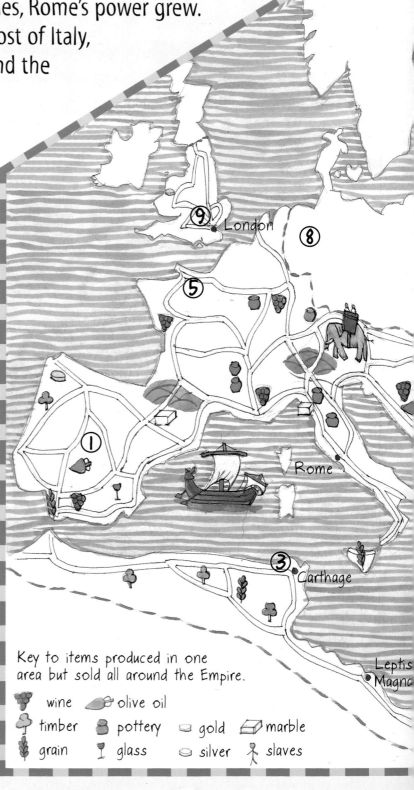

Key to items produced in one area but sold all around the Empire.

- 🍇 wine
- 🫒 olive oil
- 🌳 timber
- 🏺 pottery
- ▱ gold
- ▱ marble
- 🌾 grain
- 🍷 glass
- ▱ silver
- 🧍 slaves

Julius Caesar (100–44BC) was a Roman general who helped expand the Empire. He might have become emperor, but was murdered at the height of his power.

Pompey (106–48 BC) was another Roman general. He fought Julius Caesar for control of the Empire, but lost and was murdered soon after.

Claudius (AD10–54) was the emperor who conquered Britain. He made the Empire easier to run, too. He was murdered by his wife!

Hadrian (AD76–138) became emperor after Trajan in AD117, when the empire was at its largest. Like Claudius, he was good at running the empire. He died after a long illness.

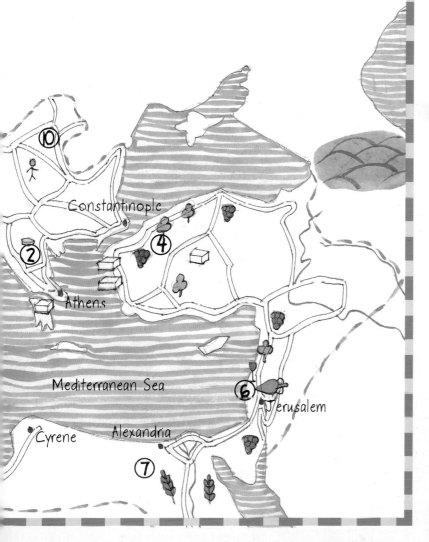

Constantinople

Athens

Mediterranean Sea

Cyrene   Alexandria

Jerusalem

⑥ Eastern Mediterranean

Pompey captures Jerusalem in 63BC. He defeats Mithridates, the powerful king of Pontus, and makes Syria a Roman province.

⑦ Egypt

In 48BC Julius Caesar meets Egypt's Queen Cleopatra. After the famous sea battle of Actium (31BC), Cleopatra kills herself and Augustus, Caesar's nephew, becomes the first Roman emperor. Egypt becomes a province.

⑧ Germany

By AD9 the Romans have taken parts of the territories that now form Germany and Austria. They never control the whole of Germany.

⑨ Britain

Emperor Claudius begins Rome's conquest of Britain in AD43. Hadrian visits Britain in AD122 and orders his army to build a huge frontier wall in the north.

⑩ Dacia (Roumania)

In AD106, the Emperor Trajan takes this region into Roman control. The Empire reaches its greatest extent under Trajan's rule.

What was life in the Empire like?

The powerful Roman army controlled the Empire and kept it peaceful. Many people grew rich during the *Pax Romana* (Roman Peace).

What made the Empire stay prosperous?

The occupying Roman armies needed feeding, so local farmers grew rich selling their produce. Towns increased in size. Trade also grew as people selling goods – raw materials, food, craft goods and luxuries – criss-crossed the old frontiers now lying within Rome's huge, growing empire.

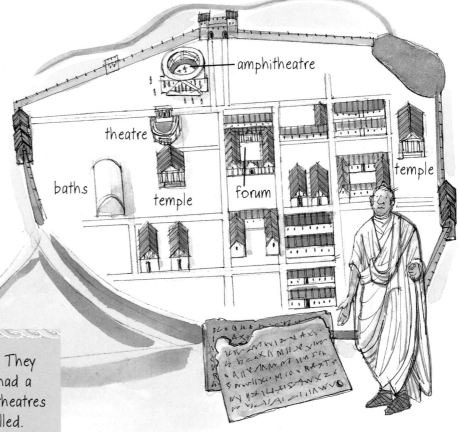

amphitheatre

theatre

baths

temple

forum

temple

Roman towns were well planned. They were built on a square grid and had a main market square (forum), amphitheatres and baths. They were often walled.

Who were Roman citizens?

Originally, Roman citizens were people who had been born in Rome. Then, as the Empire grew, important people from the provinces (countries in the Empire outside Rome) were granted citizenship, as a reward. Most people wanted to be citizens because it gave them full rights under Roman law. For example, they could serve in the army, wear togas and, best of all, help to rule themselves.

Which Roman influences spread across the Empire?

Across the Empire, people used the same coins, obeyed the same laws and paid the same taxes. People travelled on new Roman roads and saw new towns and cities built around them. Latin was the new language across the western part of the Empire. And, of course, Roman villas were built across the Empire, too.

The Emperor

He was the most powerful man in Rome. He commanded the army and appointed the senators. Many emperors were worshipped as gods after they died.

Senators

The senators were a few hundred rich men who made laws and governed the empire. The senators were based in Rome but were also governors of the outlying areas of the Empire.

Knights

Knights were the next layer down in the running of the Roman Empire. They could be the junior army commanders or procurators (tax collectors and financial administrators). Some were successful businessmen.

Ordinary Roman citizens

Roman citizens were people born in Rome, or people from other provinces who had done well under Roman rule. Many Roman citizens were soldiers, businessmen, or farmers.

Freed men

Former slaves who had been granted freedom were called freed men. Some slaves bought their freedom by saving the money their masters gave them. Freed men became Roman citizens.

Non-Roman citizens

Non-Roman citizens were the people throughout the Empire who had not earned the right to be Roman citizens. These people made up 90% of the Empire.

Slaves

Slaves were people who had been captured in battle or born into slavery. Slaves were sometimes educated people. For example, many slaves from Greece were teachers or doctors.

Many conquered peoples saw that the Roman villas were better than their own traditional houses. They wanted to show their Roman conquerors that they could be civilised, too.

How did people pay for their villas?

Most new villa owners were farmers who had made lots of money selling produce in the new markets. They used their profits to build homes in the modern, comfortable Roman-villa style. Other villa owners were people who traded successfully or ran industries like pottery and mining. They too paid for their villas with profits.

What did farmers sell?

Farmers across the Empire sold meat from their farms. Products such as wool and leather were sold too. The type of crops grown varied from place to place. In the wetter north-western provinces like Britain, lots of vegetables were grown. Then, in the hot, dry south like Spain and Italy, olives were the main crops, while in North Africa cereals and grain flourished.

Cows and sheep were kept for their milk, meat, wool and hide.

Olives were grown for their oil, used in cooking, cleaning and lamps.

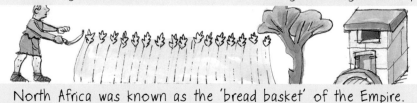

North Africa was known as the 'bread basket' of the Empire.

Why else did people build villas?

Another reason for building a villa was to show how powerful you were. Some people built huge villas, almost like palaces. In about AD75 the British king, Cogidubnus, built a palatial villa at Fishbourne, near Chichester. His villa showed people that he was rich enough to afford the best Roman luxuries. It also showed that he was a man with powerful Roman friends. He remained the local king in southern Britain even after the Roman conquest.

Welcome to my fabulous villa. Enjoy the feast!

Any more roast swan?

The magnificent villa-palace at Fishbourne was discovered in 1960. A workman was digging in farmland to lay water pipes when he cut through a layer of Roman roofing tiles! Archaeologists were called to the scene and they identified five walls, two mosaic floors and scraps of 1st century AD pottery.

At the villa, Cogidubnus could hold feasts and impress his local friends with his wealth and sophistication.

Where did you build your villa?

After the Romans invaded a new territory, the first villas were built where the Roman army presence was strong. Then, once peace was established, people built villas elsewhere too.

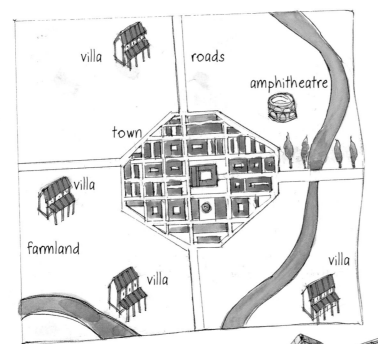

Where did farmers build their villas?

Farmers built villas where the land was fertile. A successful farm meant that there would be money for villa improvements and extra rooms. In North Africa, the villas and estates were particularly large, and irrigation schemes made the land there very productive. The farmers became among the richest in the Empire by selling their grain harvests to Rome, to feed its huge, and growing, population.

Why build near water?

A water supply was needed for kitchens, bathhouses and toilets inside the home, as well as for a fountain in the courtyard garden. To be sure of enough water, farmers sunk wells or, better still, built their home by a flowing stream. Building near a river also meant that grain could be loaded onto boats, bound for the town.

Why were country villas built near towns?

Villas generally had a town nearby. Villa-farmers needed them for the big markets where they could sell their produce. Other wealthy villa owners lived in towns most of the year. They built their country villas nearby so that they could easily go there for a holiday, or to entertain friends.

How important were Roman roads?

Wherever they conquered territory, the Romans used hundreds of slaves to build good, straight roads. These roads allowed people and goods to travel quickly and safely around the Empire. Most villas were built near roads. The five essential stages in road-building were as follows:

1. Surveying the course of the road.
2. Clearing away vegetation and levelling the track.
3. Laying the foundations – using large or small stones.
4. Laying the surface.
5. Digging a ditch on either side, for drainage.

Why build a villa by the sea?

Some wealthy Romans chose to build their villas by the sea, near the Bay of Naples. These villas had columns at the front, and jetties built out into the sea. The location, in south-west Italy, was on an extremely beautiful coastline, with fertile farming land nearby.

Who were the builders?

When the army had conquered a new land, they set about restoring peace and establishing Roman rule. Soon after, architects, craftsmen and artists arrived from other parts of the Empire.

How were the villas designed?

People who wished to build villas would generally employ an architect to draw up the plans. Architects knew the very latest fashions in Rome, and were able to incorporate these into a villa's design. They also knew their rich clients would be ready to pay for the very best materials, such as fine marble imported from Greece and Italy.

Carpenters

Carpenters had plenty of work to do on site. Before building work began, they made the scaffolding and the framework. Then, as the building work got under way, they sawed timber for the walls and the roof. Finally, they put wooden floors in the less important rooms.

Craftsmen crossed frontiers around the Empire, taking the same architectural details to places as far afield as Spain, Britain and North Africa.

Mosaic artists

These craftsmen used tiny stone cubes called *tesserae* to make patterns and pictures. They sometimes added glass, pottery or tile pieces for a special effect. The best mosaics were reserved for a villa's most important reception rooms, where owners entertained their guests.

mosaics

wall painting ▶

frieze ▼

Plaster-workers

Most walls inside a Roman villa were covered with smooth, painted plaster. But some of the grandest villa rooms were decorated with plaster mouldings. Some mouldings were friezes, which ran between the walls and the ceilings. Others covered the whole wall.

Stonemasons

Stonemasons used a combination of local stone and expensive imports to create statues, pillars and other decorative elements. All the best craftsmen knew the classical Roman styles. They set a high standard for local sculptors to follow.

Wall-painters

They created beautiful paintings on the plaster walls using paints made of beeswax mixed with colour pigments. Some of the best examples were found in Pompeii, a Roman town in southern Italy, which was buried by a volcanic eruption in AD79.

Potters

Potters used local clay to make the thousands of clay tiles that were needed to roof villas and to make hypocausts (see page 20). Bricks were also made from clay. The clay was put into moulds first, then left to dry before being fired in the kilns.

How were the villas built?

The style of a Roman villa changed through time, and varied across the Empire. However, the building techniques involved were generally the same.

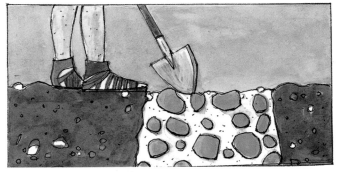

First, the builders dug trenches for the foundations. These would be filled with stoney rubble and cement to make a firm concrete base.

Concrete was an important Roman invention. It was made from heated limestone, water and sand. Volcanic ash was added to make it waterproof.

Next they constructed the walls. Some were made of tiles or of stone with a rubble core. Others had timber frames filled with wattle and daub (plaster).

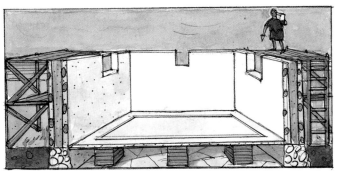

Tile pillars supported the floors of important rooms. This allowed room for the hypocausts – the underfloor heating systems (see page 20).

Builders needed wooden scaffolding so that they could work on the upper storey of the villa and its roof.

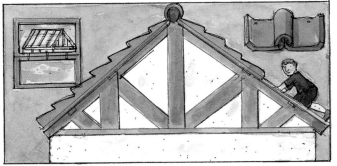

The roof completed the villa's construction. Builders fitted timber rafters to the top of the walls, and covered these frames with clay tiles.

How did villas vary across the Empire?

There were many styles of villa around the Empire, even within one country. Some, like the cottage villa, were simple buildings. Others were larger, more extravagant buildings, like the aisled villas and courtyard villas illustrated below.

Aisled villas

Two rows of pillars supported the roof of these villas and divided the building into one big hall with two aisles (corridors) – just like the design of a Roman basilica (see panel). The hall itself could be divided into many rooms. These villas often looked like grand churches, with high stone walls and a huge roof.

> Roman basilicas were like town halls, built on the forum (market place) in a town centre. Some later basilicas were adapted to become churches.

Courtyard villas

The grandest farm-villas turned the space at the front of the house into a formal courtyard. Visitors had to pass through the front gateway and cross the courtyard to reach the main house.

How were the villas heated?

Baths and hypocaust heating systems were some of the most sophisticated features of the Roman villas. Before the Romans arrived, few places in the Empire had seen such luxury and comfort.

What was a hypocaust?

A hypocaust was an underfloor heating system. Villas in the colder parts of the Roman Empire needed winter heating, especially in living rooms that had stone floors. From the 1st century AD, more and more villa owners built hypocausts under the floors of their most important rooms. They were then able to stay warm in the coldest weather.

As well as hypocausts, the Romans used charcoal braziers – metal containers holding burning charcoal for heat. Fumes from the braziers nearly killed Emperor Julian (AD361-363), and did kill Emperor Jovian in AD364.

How did a hypocaust work?

Before they built the floor, builders put stacks of tiles underneath to support it. Then they built a wood-burning furnace onto an outside wall. When it was lit (and kept alight by slaves) it gave out hot air that was channelled under the floor. Having done its job heating the floor, the hot air then flowed through flues (chimneys) in the four walls and was allowed to escape out of the roof.

Slaves worked hard to keep the wood-burning furnace alight.

What were Roman baths?

By the 1st century BC, most towns in Italy had public baths. Later, the best villas had them, too. The baths were designed as a place for the owner to relax with friends.

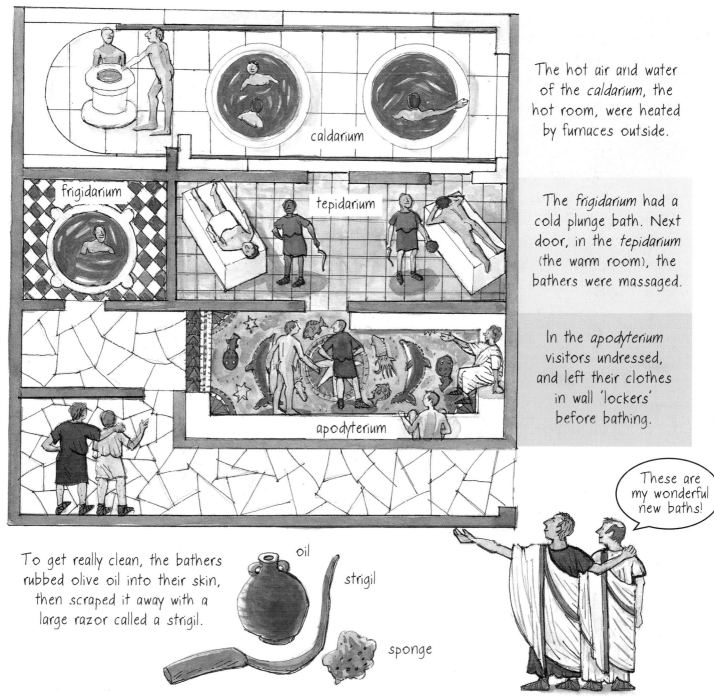

The hot air and water of the *caldarium*, the hot room, were heated by furnaces outside.

The *frigidarium* had a cold plunge bath. Next door, in the *tepidarium* (the warm room), the bathers were massaged.

In the *apodyterium* visitors undressed, and left their clothes in wall 'lockers' before bathing.

caldarium

frigidarium

tepidarium

apodyterium

These are my wonderful new baths!

To get really clean, the bathers rubbed olive oil into their skin, then scraped it away with a large razor called a strigil.

oil

strigil

sponge

How did you decorate your villa?

Rich villa owners paid a lot of money to make their homes beautiful. Outside, the courtyard gardens were filled with wonderful plants and sculptures. Inside, magnificent craftwork covered the ceilings, walls and floors.

We simply must have a statue in our courtyard garden!

colonnaded walkways

In the villa's courtyard, colonnaded walkways gave shelter from the sun or rain. People would stroll along these open corridors admiring the garden through the pillars. Pillars were usually made of stone. Their tops, or capitols, were decorated in various styles – from the simple Doric to the elaborate Composite.

Courtyard gardens were beautiful places to relax in. They would often contain neat hedges, herb and flower gardens as well as statues and carvings. Some plants that the Romans grew are still grown in gardens today.

Doric

Ionic

Corinthian

Composite

Opus sectile floors

This Latin name described pictures made up of thinly-cut pieces of coloured marble. It was a very expensive technique and was used only for a building's most important floors. In this example from Rome, a tiger is attacking a terrified calf.

Wall paintings

Villa owners often chose popular Roman subjects for their wall paintings. Scenes from nature, like gardens, flowers and birds, were especially popular. Some of the best examples can be seen at Pompeii, in southern Italy. The volcanic ash that buried the town has kept some villa walls in nearly perfect condition and the colours remain almost as bright as they were in AD79.

What pictures were used in mosaics?

Black and white geometric patterns (squares, crosses, diamonds and triangles) were very fashionable in mosaics in the 1st century AD. Later, the mosaics contained pictures. Villa owners would choose the subject that they wanted, for example the natural world, mythical creatures or gods. Top quality mosaics showed off the owner's wealth, taste and learning.

How did you live in your villa?

We know that most Roman villas had plenty of decoration… but only a little furniture. Archaeologists have sifted through evidence on many villa sites, looking to see how people lived in Roman times.

The triclinium

Banquets held in the *triclinium* were an important part of villa life. The host used them as opportunities to show off his great wealth. People ate their meals lying down on couches while slaves served the three-course meals on beautiful silver trays. Dormice and roast swan were special favourites! Guests were treated to entertainments such as juggling, dance, music and singing.

The kitchens

Large villas had many servants and slaves to help on the farm and in the house. The kitchen was a bustling place where many of them worked together. They prepared meals for the family and for banquet guests, cooking in metal pots and pans over a charcoal fire.

Menu of the Day
1st course
Snails fattened with milk, dormouse stuffed with pork & pine kernels, jellyfish & eggs.
2nd course
Roast parrot, roast swan, roast boar stuffed with thrushes, boiled flamingo & dates.
3rd course
Honey cakes, stuffed dates

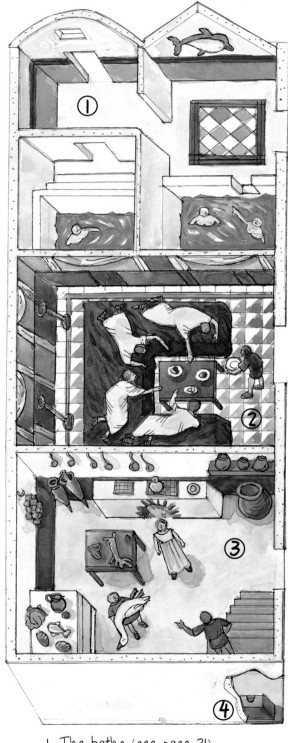

1. The baths (see page 21)
2. The trinclinium
3. The kitchens
4. The lavatory
5. The apodyterium (see page 21)

The lavatory

The lavatory was a wooden or stone seat placed over a sewer. Sponges and running water were supplied.

The courtyard garden

This was a private area of the house where the family could relax. Herbs and flowers grew here, and fountains and statues were popular garden features.

The living room

The living room furniture was simple and there was not much of it. But a rich villa owner could afford beautiful marble or mosaic floors, heated from below. In an ornate room such as this, he would entertain important guests.

The atrium

The atrium was the villa's entrance hall. In it was the lararium shrine that honoured the *lares* and the *penates*, who were household gods. The lares were the family's guardians and the penates were suppposed to keep the cellar full of food and wine!

lararium

lares and penates

6. The courtyard garden
7. The living room
8. Atrium containing the lararium shrine
9. A bedroom (there were more upstairs)

What happened to the Empire?

In the second and third centuries AD, Rome's great Empire began to weaken. The huge army was costly to keep, taxes rose and there were too few slaves to work the land. The Empire had become too big to control.

Why did the Empire divide?

By the end of the 3rd century AD, after decades of economic troubles and barbarian invasions, the huge Roman Empire became ungovernable. Emperor Diocletian divided it into eastern and western halves, and shared power with three other leaders. These changes kept the Empire going for another 170 years.

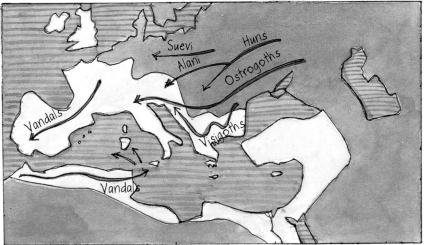

In the 5th century barbarian invaders (outsiders from the north and east) successfully attacked and overcame Rome and its Western Empire.

Why did people leave their villas?

As Rome's Western Empire weakened, the Roman army began to pull out. People were left alone to defend themselves against the invading barbarians. As a result most people abandoned their country villas and fled to the safety of the towns. British villa-life still prospered for a while. In fact, in Britain during the 4th century AD more villas were built than ever before. But when invaders, slaves and even poor neighbours became a threat, the last villas were abandoned too. By AD460 the era of the villas had ended.

26

the Pont du Gard ▼

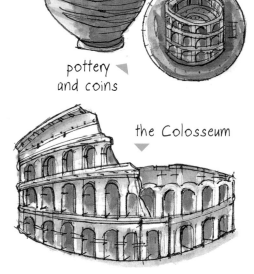

pottery
and coins ◄

the Colosseum ▼

What remains of the Roman Empire?

The Roman Empire may have ended, but it is not forgotten. There are many fine buildings still standing, such as amphitheatres, aqueducts and temples. These are scattered all over the former Empire. Archaeologists have discovered much more too — magnificent mosaic floors, pots, coins, treasure hoards... and even the preserved shapes of people and animals who lived and died in Pompeii, buried by Vesuvius's volcanic ash.

a dead dog buried at Pompeii ▼

theatre at Leptis Magna

What sites do tourists visit?

Many of these Roman buildings are big tourist attractions — for example the Colosseum in Rome, the Pont du Gard in the south of France, Hadrian's Villa at Tivoli, the Roman baths at Bath in England and the magnificent theatre at Leptis Magna in North Africa. People also visit the remains of villas and houses, such as those found in and around Pompeii.

mosaics from Fishbourne Palace ▲

What are archaeologists doing today ?

Archaeologists continue to work on all these sites and, with their modern technology, discover more and more about life in the Roman Empire.

Hadrian's Wall still stands along the northern frontier of the Roman Empire in Britain

Vindolanda tablet found near Hadrian's Wall ▶

Timeline

753BC The legendary Romulus founds Rome.

509BC The Temple of Jupiter is built on the Capitol, in Rome.

c.272BC Rome rules most of Italy.

185BC Rome begins town planning.

58-51BC Caesar invades France and Britain.

44 BC Julius Caesar is assassinated.

AD43 Claudius invades Britain unopposed.

61 Queen Boudica revolts against Romans in Britain.

98-117 The Roman Empire is at its biggest, under Emperor Trajan.

113 Trajan's Column is built in Rome.

122-127 Hadrian's Wall is built along the northern frontier in Britain.

130-38 Hadrian builds a magnificent villa at Tivoli.

212 All free men are granted Roman citizenship.

c 250 Barbarian invasions. Rome's European provinces attacked.

313 Emperor Constantine tolerates the new religion, Christianity.

330 Constantinople is declared the new capital of the Empire.

c.370s-mid 400s More barbarian tribes attack.

395 The Roman Empire is split in two.

410 Rome is captured and looted.

449 Tribes from Northern Europe invade Britain.

476 The Western Roman Empire comes to an end.

Glossary

amphitheatre
An open-air oval-shaped theatre with stepped seating. Gladiator and other entertainment shows took place here.

archaeologist
A person who digs up and studies the remains of buildings and objects from the past to find out about the people who made them.

architect
A person who designs buildings.

barbarian
An outsider, someone from outside the Empire, particularly from the north and east, such as the Franks and the Visigoths.

forum
The central square and market place of a Roman town or city.

foundations
The base on which a building is constructed.

governor
The ruler of a province, an area of the Empire, such as Egypt.

hypocaust
Underfloor central heating system used in Roman villas.

procurator
A financial agent or tax collector for a province.

province
One the areas of land, such as Egypt or Gaul (France), that the Romans divided their Empire into so that they could run it more easily.

senator
A member of the Senate, the ruling body of the Roman Empire.

tax
The money or goods which people pay to their government or their ruler.

territory
The whole or part of the land occupied by the Roman Empire.

triclinium
The Roman (Latin) name for a dining room in a Roman villa.

Index

archaeologist 6, 13, 24, 27
architect 16
army 7, 8, 9, 10, 11, 14, 16, 26
artist 16, 17
atrium 25

barbarian 26, 28
baths 10, 20, 21, 27
bathhouse 6, 14
Britain 6, 9, 12, 13, 16, 26, 27, 28
businessman 7, 11

Caesar, Julius 8, 9, 28
carpenter 16
citizen 7, 10, 11
Claudius 9, 28
Cogidubnus 13
courtyard 6, 14, 19, 22, 25
craftsman 16-17

decoration 17, 22-23, 24

emperor 9, 11, 20, 26

farmer 7, 10, 11, 12, 14, 15
Fishbourne Palace 13, 27
forum 10, 19

garden 14, 22, 25
Gaul 8, 28
Germany 9, 16
god 11, 23, 25
Greece 6, 8, 11, 16

Hadrian 9, 27
Hadrian's Wall 9, 27, 28

hypocaust 17, 18, 20

Italy 7, 8, 12, 15, 16, 17, 23, 28

kitchen 14, 24

lararium shrine 25
lavatory 14, 24, 25
living room 25

mosaic 6, 13, 17, 23, 25, 27

North Africa 8, 12, 14, 16, 27

plaster-worker 17
Pompeii 7, 17, 23, 27
Pompey 8, 9
potter 17

road 10, 15
Rome 6, 7, 8, 9, 10, 11, 14, 16, 23, 26, 27, 28

senator 11
slave 11, 15, 20, 24, 26
Spain 8, 12
stonemason 17

town 7, 10, 14, 15, 17, 19, 21, 26
tradesman 7, 10
Trajan 9, 28
triclinium 24

wall painting 17, 23